# S'UPID SH*T YOU SAY

## BRAD GOSSE

DEDICATION

FOR ELAINE, SONIA AND MEERA. THANKS FOR REMINDING ME TO LAUGH EVERY DAY AND NOT TAKE THINGS TOO SERIOUSLY.

*The things we say to each other at home, work and on social media are mean, funny, aggressive and sometimes stupid.*

*My name is Brad Gosse. I have no credentials.*

*In 2012 I wrote an alternative business book about online marketing and I speak about that topic around the world.*

*Along the way I've witnessed the crazy stuff we say online and off that make other people cringe. So I catalogued them here in this easy to digest book.*

*If you say some of the things in this book stop it.*

*If someone gave you thing book, ask yourself why and take some time to reflect on your words.*

*Enjoy this book.*
*Share it with someone who needs it.*

*If you want to reach me.*

*TW: @bradgosse*
*IG: @bradgosse*
*FB: @bradgosse*

ASKING FOR PRAYERS

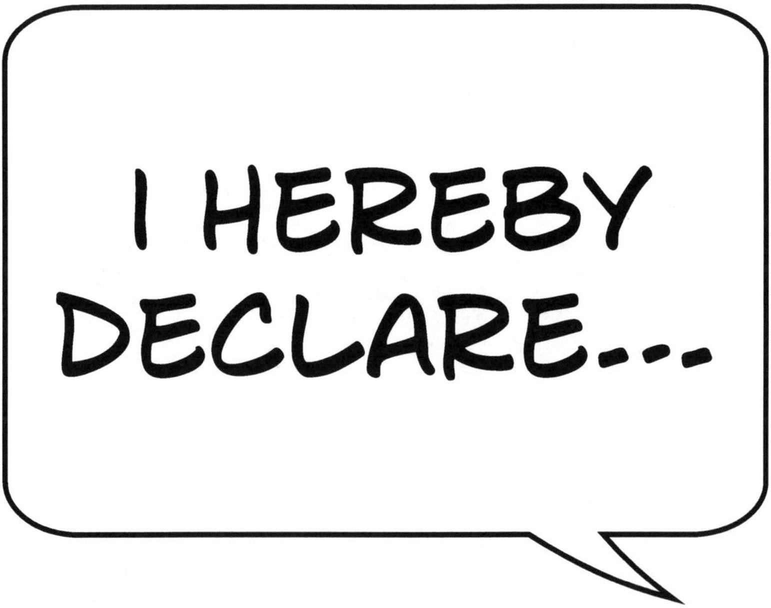
I HEREBY DECLARE...

# MY PHONE IS LISTENING TO ME.

# BURPEES

KARMA

I'M HOPING THE UNIVERSE WILL DELIVER ME A....

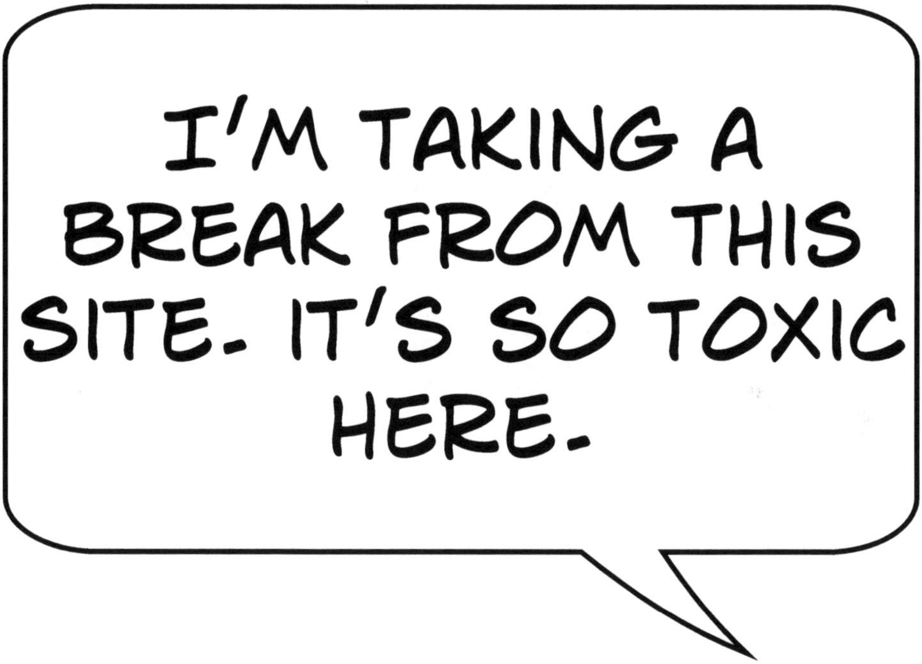
I'M TAKING A BREAK FROM THIS SITE. IT'S SO TOXIC HERE.

BUSY. BUSY. BUSY.

# CASH IN ON YOUR PASSION

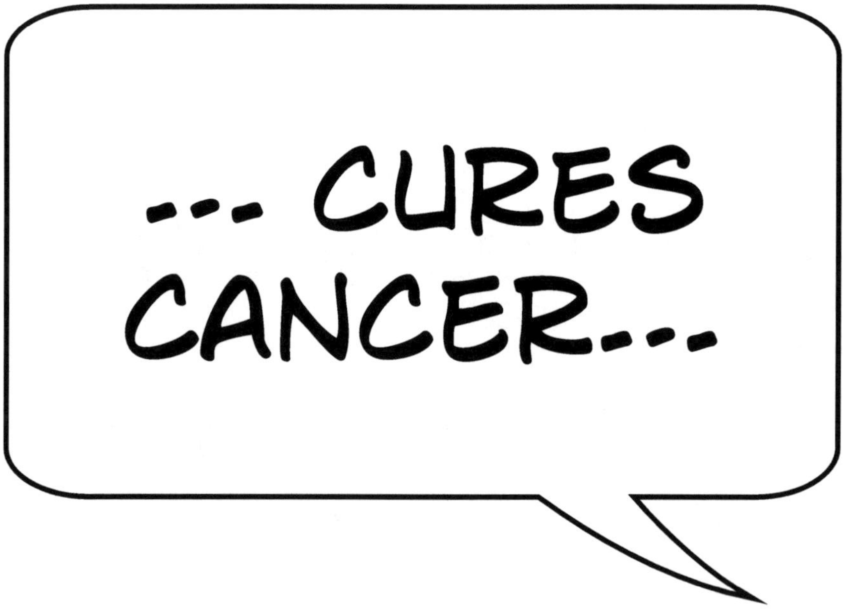
... CURES CANCER...

MY WHY

# WEALTH COACH

# HUSTLE

WANTREPRENEUR

IRREGARDLESS

# NUTRACEUTICAL

DON'T SHARE THIS. COPY AND PASTE...

THINKING OF
YOU AT THIS
DIFFICULT TIME

TRY NOT TO THINK ABOUT IT

BE CAREFUL

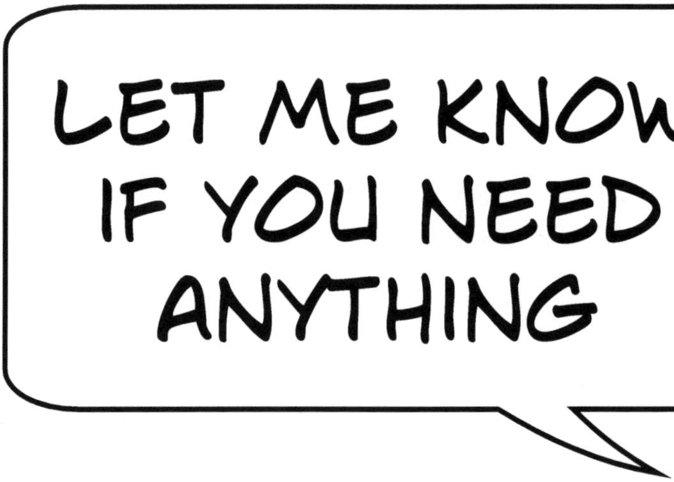
LET ME KNOW IF YOU NEED ANYTHING

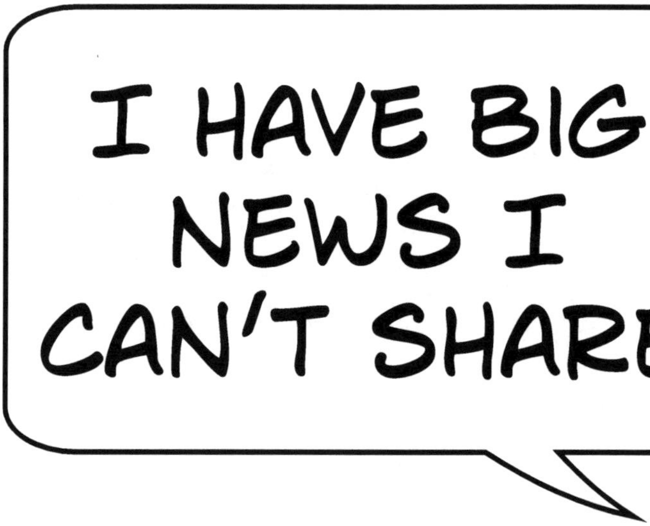
I HAVE BIG NEWS I CAN'T SHARE

NETWORKING

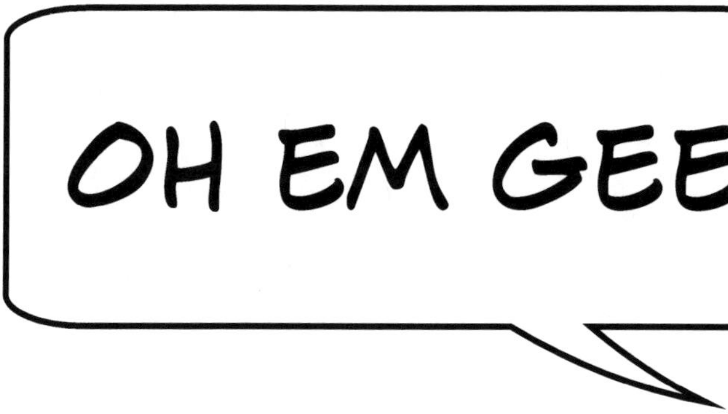
OH EM GEE

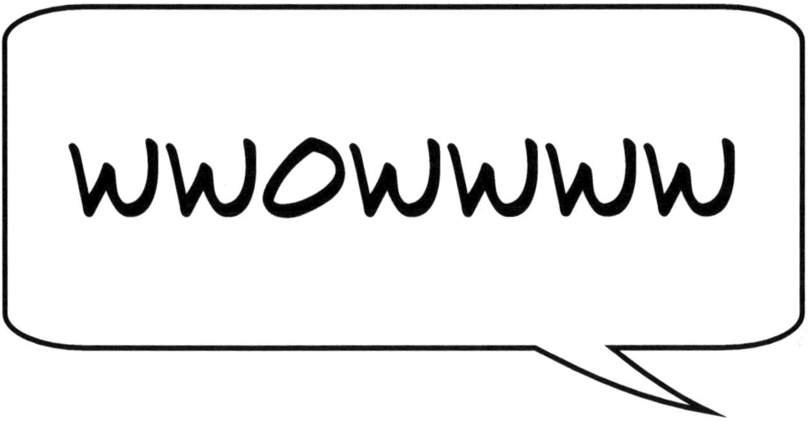
WWOWWWW

I'M JUST
GONNA PLAY
DEVILS
ADVOCATE

THINKING OF BUYING OR SELLING YOUR HOME?

STRATEGY SESSION

NOT ALL
HERO'S
WEAR CAPES

# KEEPING YOU IN MY THOUGHTS

# FIRST WORLD PROBLEMS

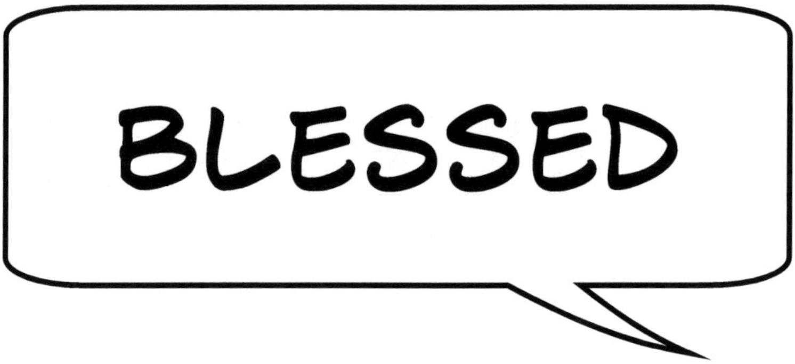
BLESSED

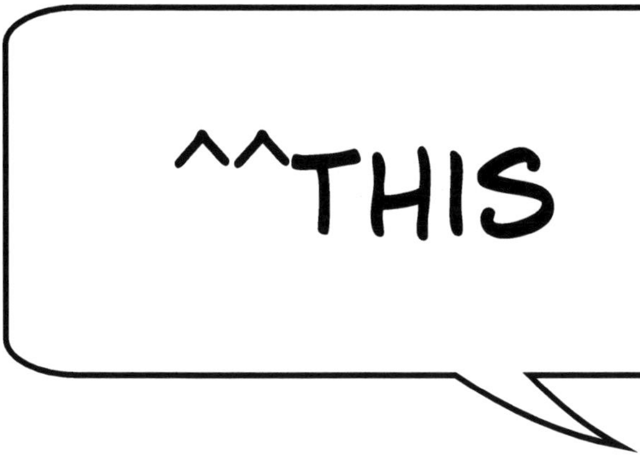
^^THIS

# INFLUENCER

WORKS AT:
INTERNET
MARKETING

# FORWARD THINKING

# THE STRUGGLE IS REAL

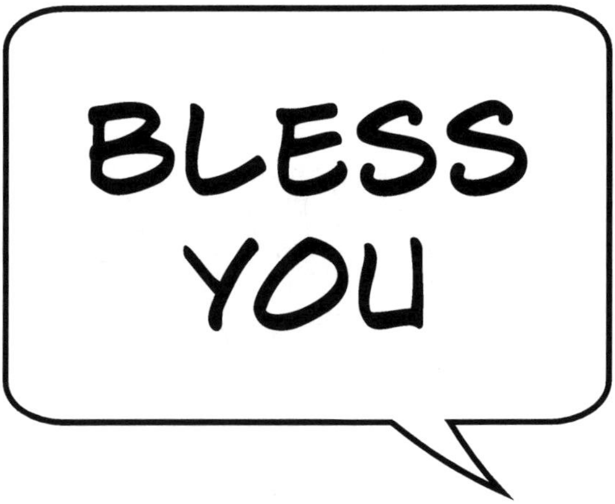
BLESS YOU

# SELF CARE

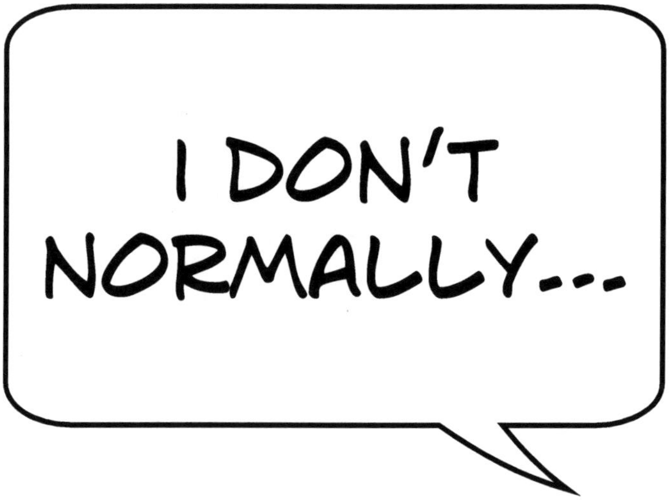
I DON'T NORMALLY...

TEN
THOUSAND
HOURS

PLEASE SEND GOOD VIBES

I JUST GAVE MONEY TO A HOMELESS PERSON.

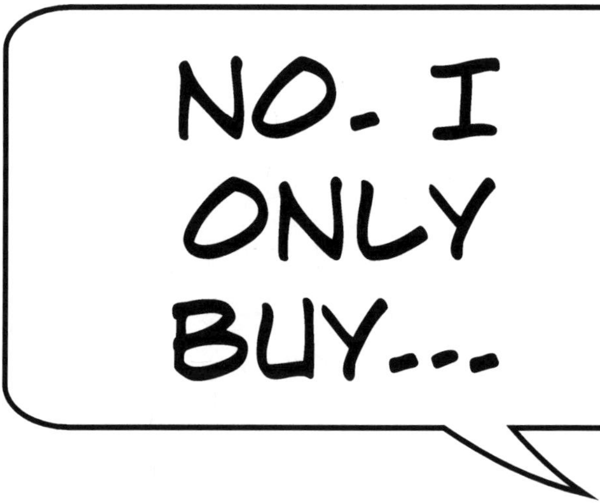
NO. I ONLY BUY...

COPY, PASTE AND TAG A FRIEND

I'M DELETING FRIENDS TODAY. COMMENT BELOW TO BE SPARED.

MY THOUGHTS AND PRAYERS GO OUT TO THE VICTIMS OF THE TRAGEDY IN...

THE PROCESS
BEFORE THE PIE

# RELATIONSHIPS ARE HARD WORK

THEY WERE LUCKY

FORGIVE EVERYTHING

# STEP BY STEP PROCESS

CHESTERFIELD

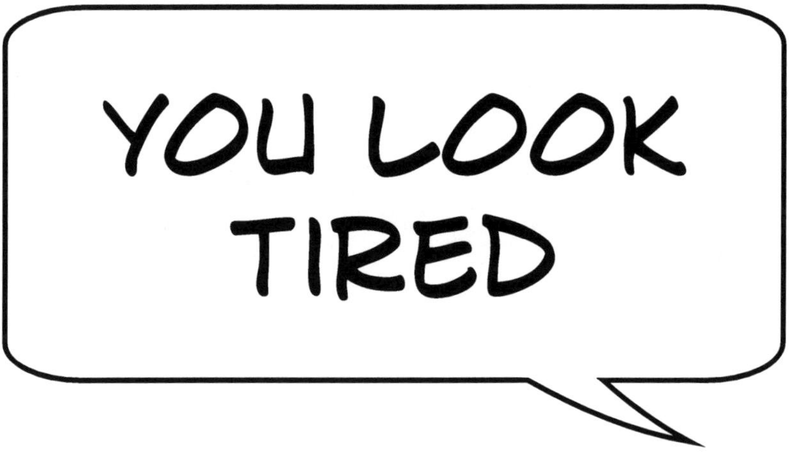
YOU LOOK TIRED

YOU LOOK
LIKE YOU'VE
PUT ON
WEIGHT

I CAN'T DO THIS FOR EVERYONE BUT...

# IS NOW A GOOD TIME TO TALK?

THE DEVIL IS
IN THE
DETAILS

TOXINS

LITERALLY

ABUNDANCE

DRIVE SAFE

RETAIL
THERAPY

# SYNERGY

FAILING TO PLAN IS PLANNING TO FAIL.

EVERYTHING
WILL WORK
OUT

GET WHAT YOU
WANT BY HELPING
OTHERS GET WHAT
THEY WANT

DADDY DAUGHTER DATE NIGHT

# MERCURY RETROGRADE

SUPPOSEBLY

HEY GUYS

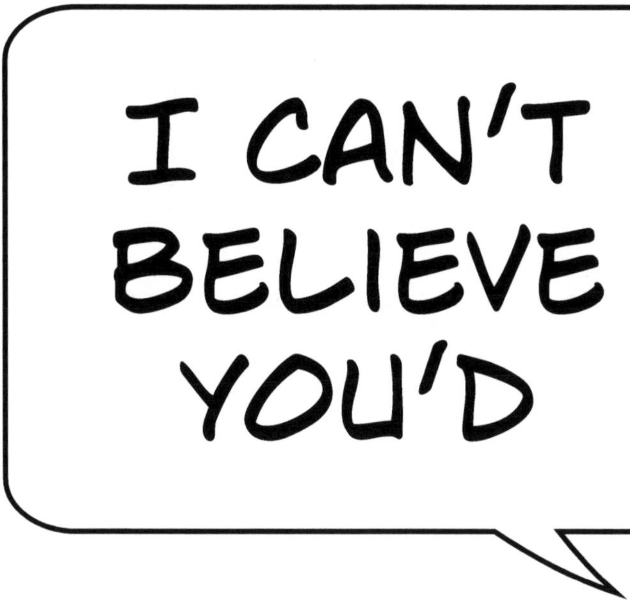
I CAN'T BELIEVE YOU'D

I DON'T MEAN
TO SOUND
JUDGMENTAL,
BUT...

IT IS WHAT
IT IS.

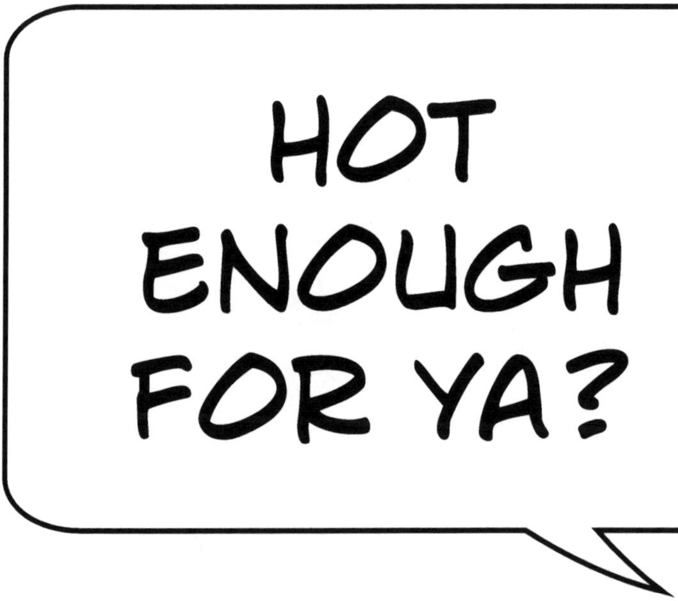
HOT ENOUGH FOR YA?

INSTAGRAM MODEL

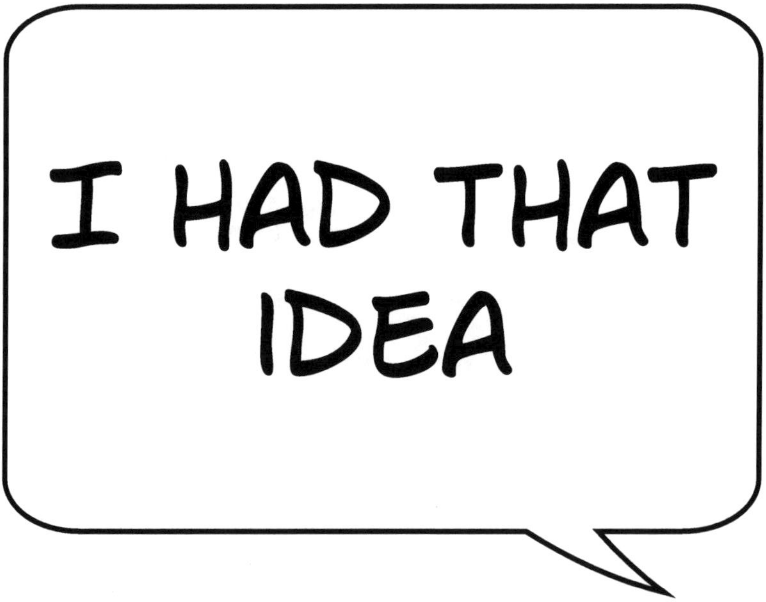
I HAD THAT IDEA

THE CAT'S ASS

SELLING
LIKE
HOTCAKES

# TRAVEL LIFESTYLE

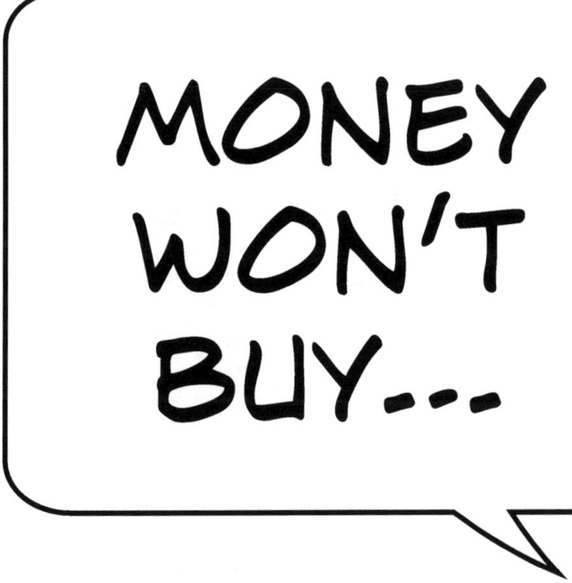
MONEY WON'T BUY...

# LET ME SPEAK TO YOUR SUPERVISOR

HANG ON LET
ME GET A
PICTURE FOR
MY INSTAGRAM

AMAZEBALLS

ETHNIC
FOOD

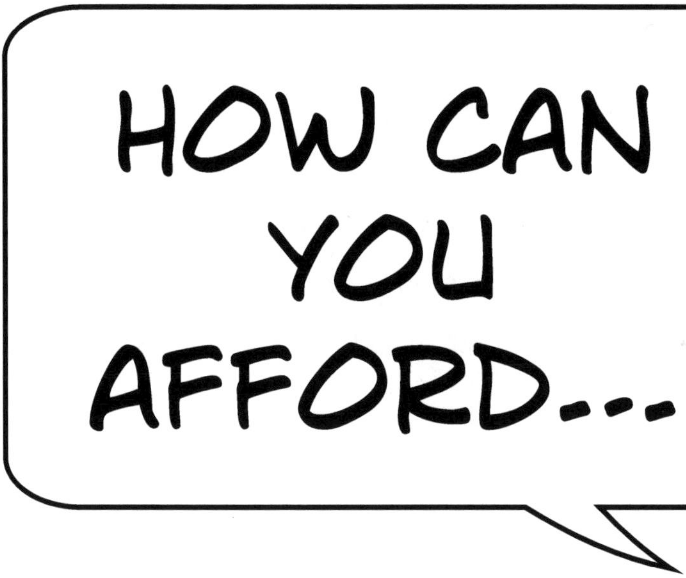
HOW CAN YOU AFFORD...

I DON'T
MEAN TO
INTERRUPT...

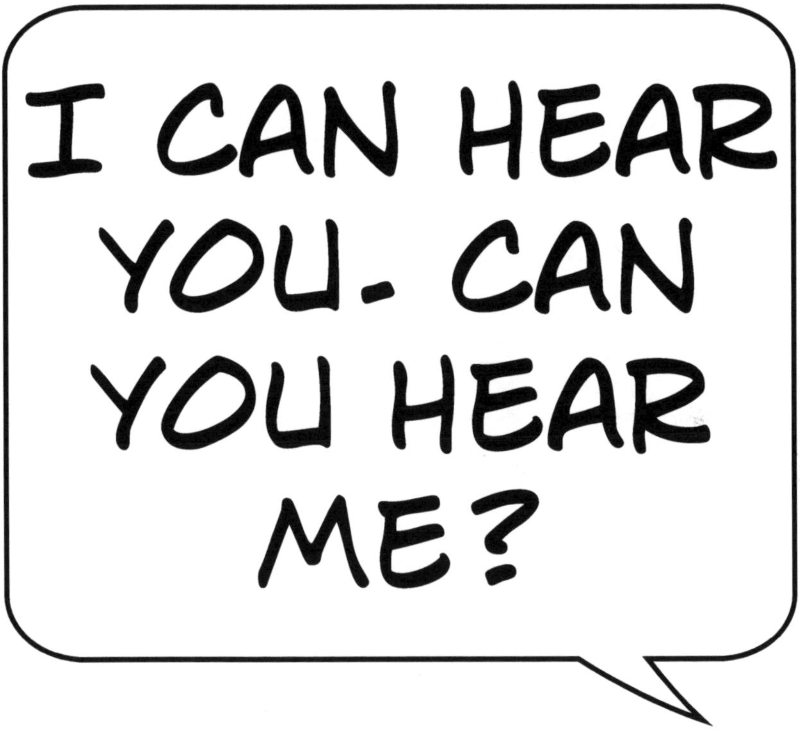
I CAN HEAR YOU. CAN YOU HEAR ME?

# I COULDN'T HELP OVERHEARING

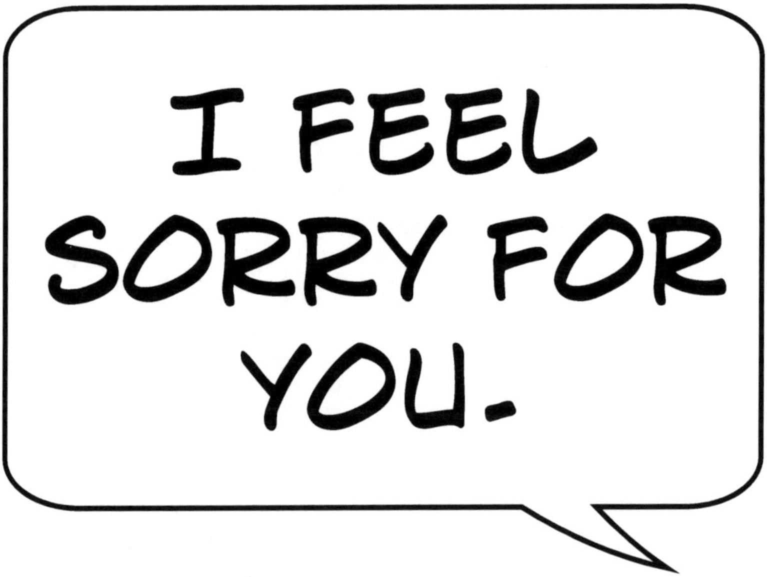
I FEEL SORRY FOR YOU.

# MONEY DOESN'T GROW ON TREES

IT'S
DARKEST
BEFORE THE
DAWN

# LOOK ON THE BRIGHT SIDE

GOOD THINGS COME TO THOSE WHO WAIT

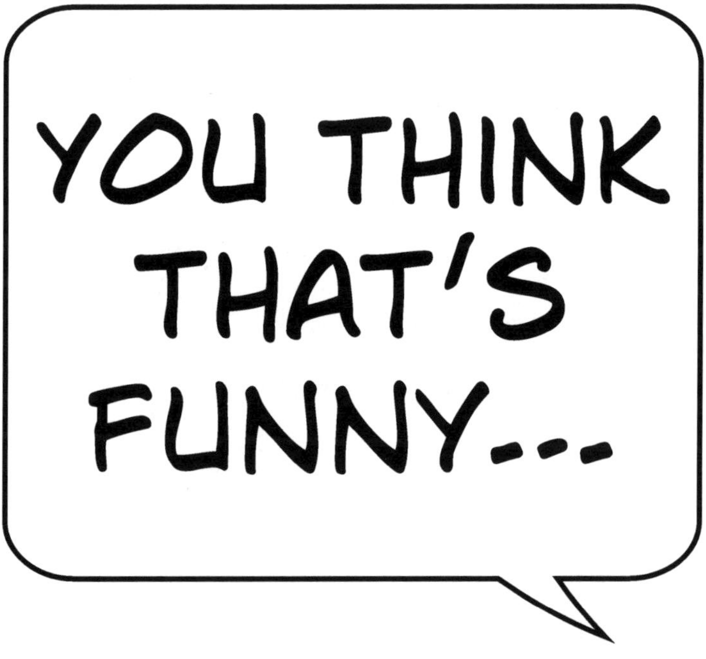
YOU THINK THAT'S FUNNY...

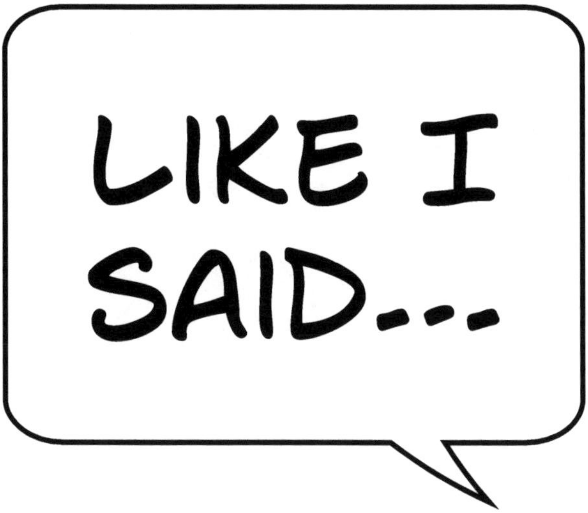
LIKE I SAID...

WHEN ARE YOU EXPECTING?

SENSE OF
ENTITLEMENT

IT'S A
DOGGY DOG
WORLD

BUTT
NAKED

# FOR ALL INTENSIVE PURPOSES

ONE IN
THE SAME

162

BECKON CALL

TOUCH
BASE
WITH...

...THINGS HAPPEN IN 3'S

MILLENNIALS

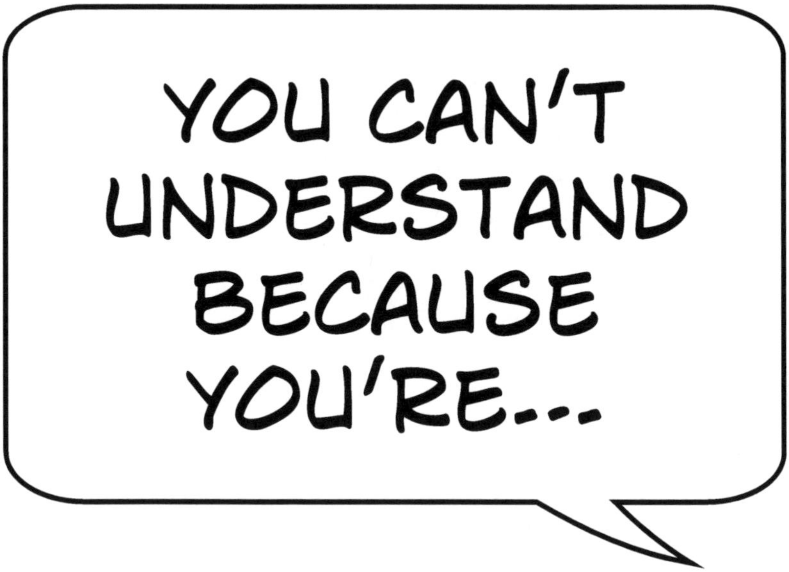
YOU CAN'T UNDERSTAND BECAUSE YOU'RE...

YOU'RE GOING
TO HAVE TO
MAKE
SACRIFICES

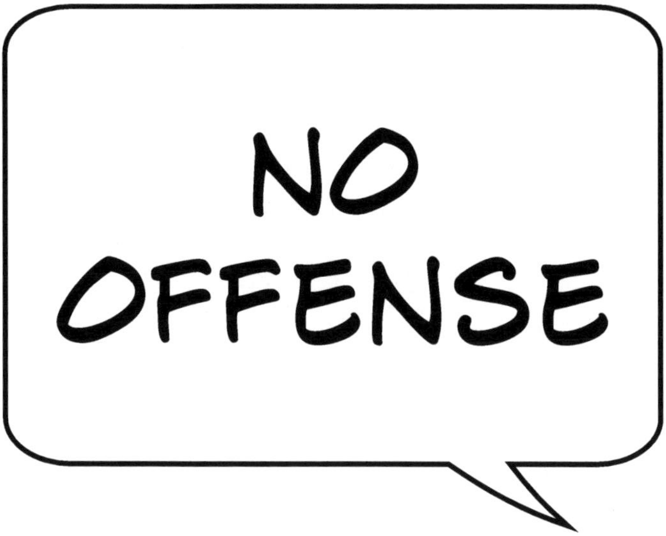
NO
OFFENSE

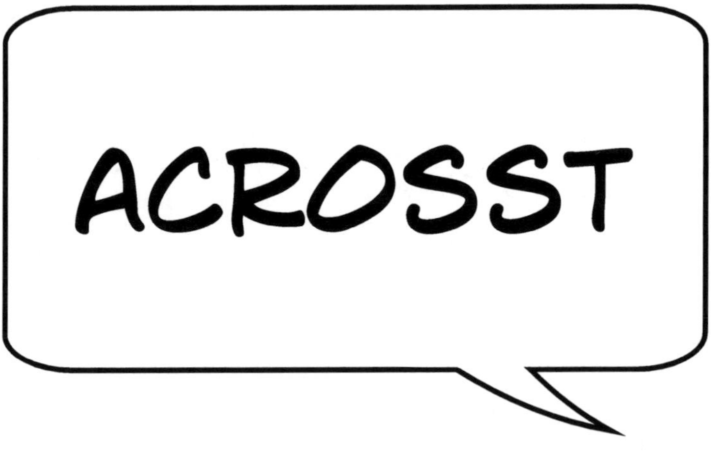
ACROSST

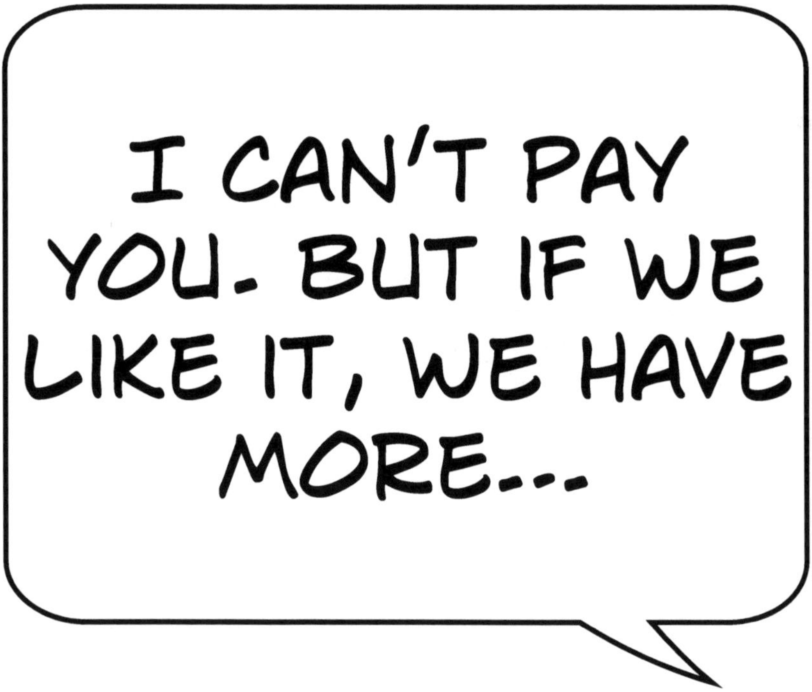
I CAN'T PAY YOU. BUT IF WE LIKE IT, WE HAVE MORE...

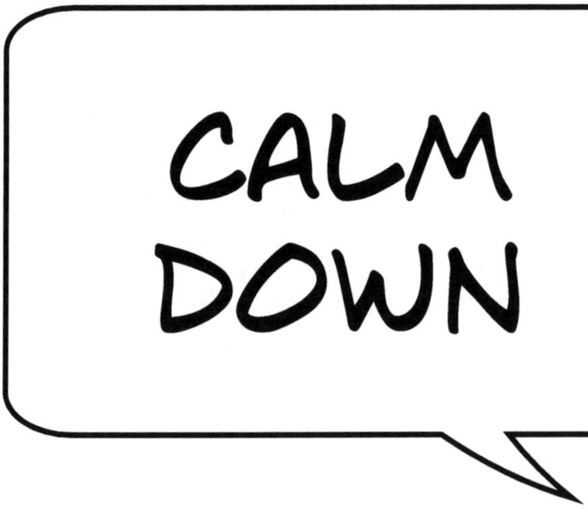
CALM DOWN

I REALLY
SHOULDN'T...

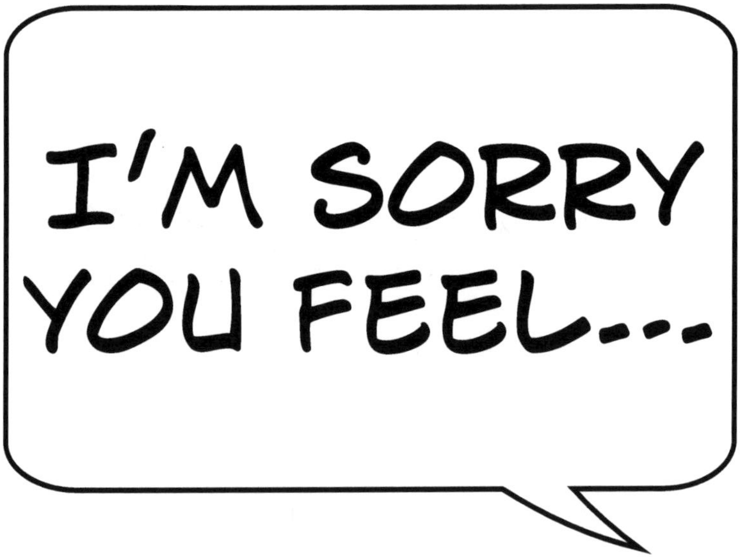
I'M SORRY YOU FEEL...

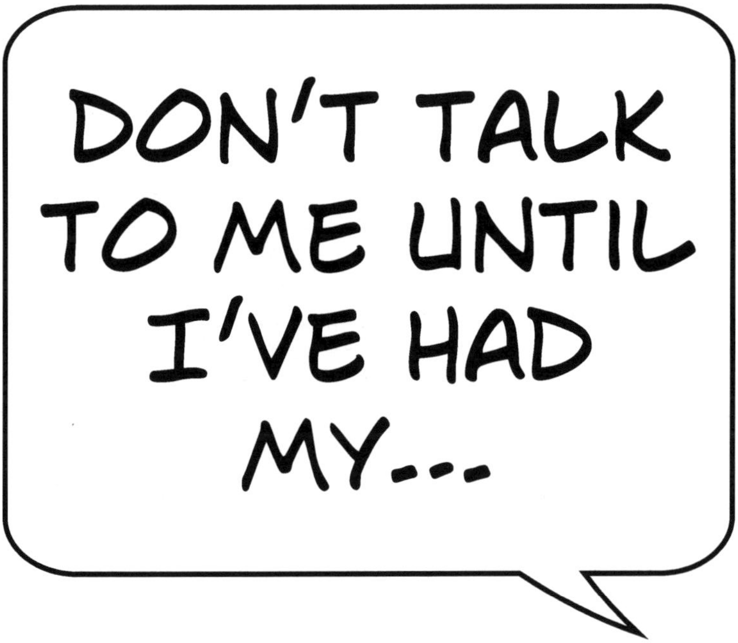
DON'T TALK TO ME UNTIL I'VE HAD MY...

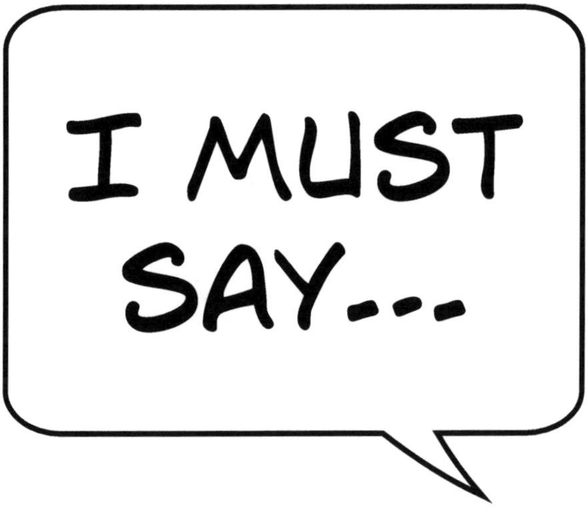
I MUST SAY...

OH AND ONE MORE THING...

CAN YOU BELIEVE THIS WEATHER?

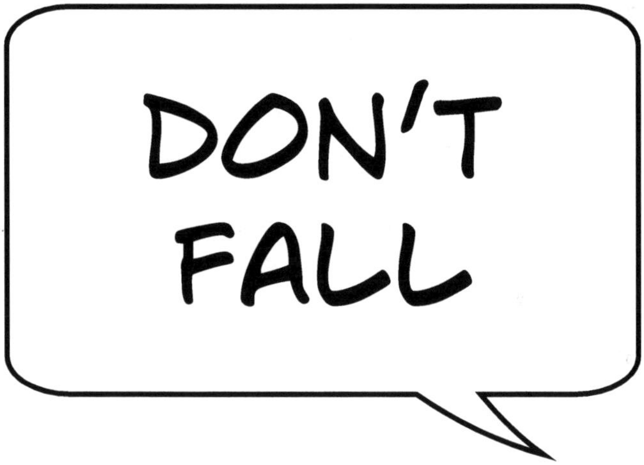
DON'T
FALL

# LAW OF ATTRACTION

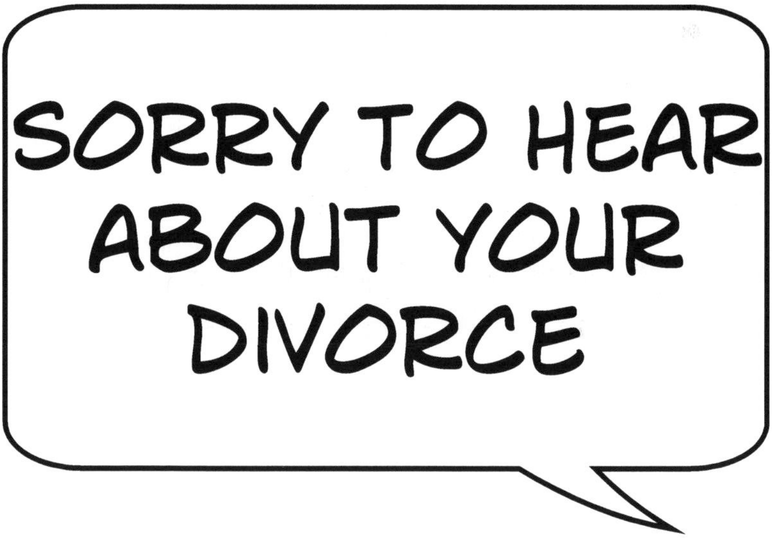
SORRY TO HEAR ABOUT YOUR DIVORCE

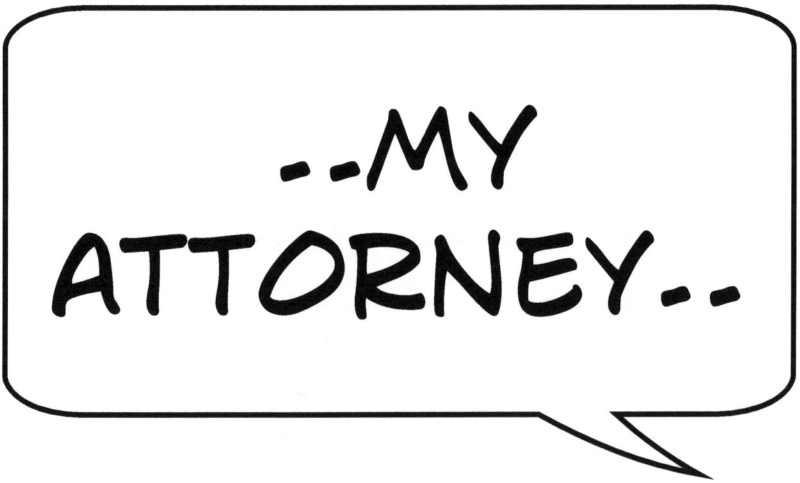
..MY ATTORNEY..

THE
CUSTOMER
IS ALWAYS
RIGHT

HOW WAS THE TRAFFIC?

MASSEUSE

EXPRESSO

WHEN A DOOR CLOSES A WINDOW OPENS

# CALORIES

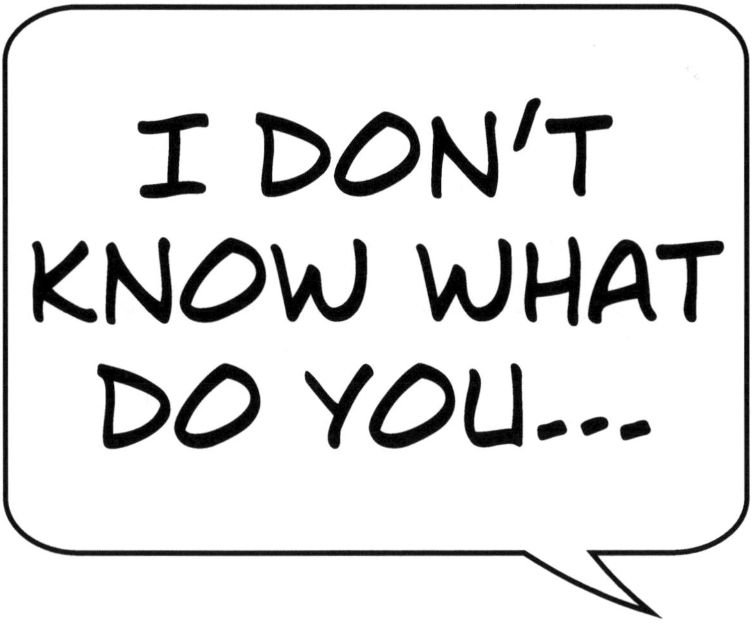
I DON'T KNOW WHAT DO YOU...

# YOU LOOK HEALTHY

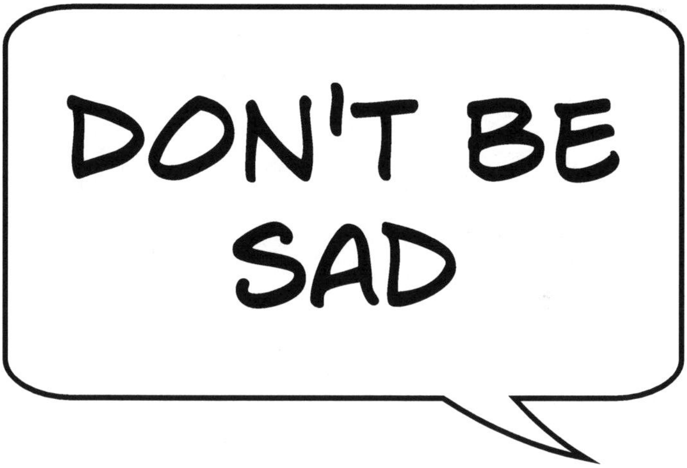
DON'T BE SAD

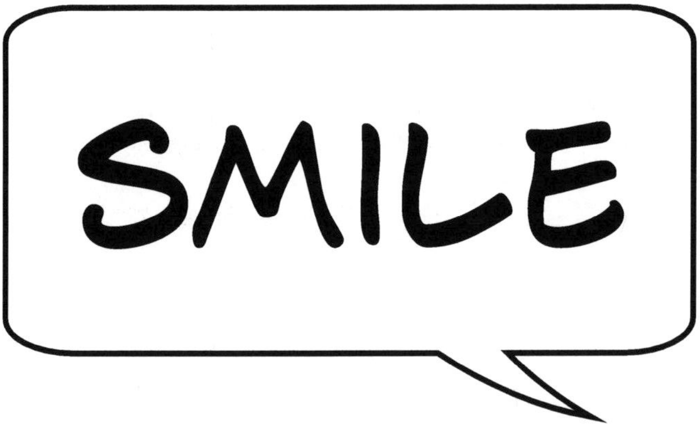
SMILE

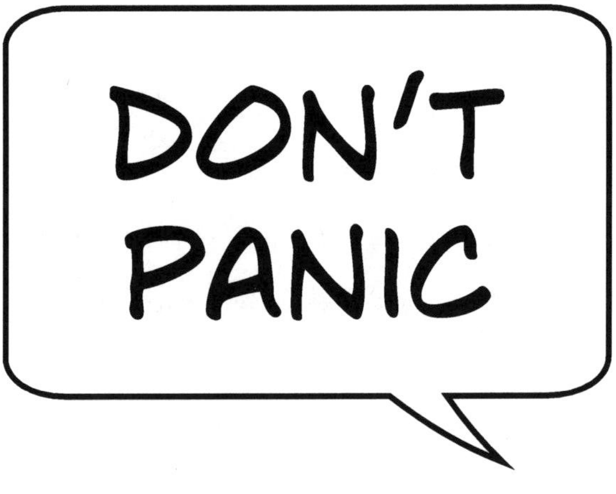
DON'T PANIC

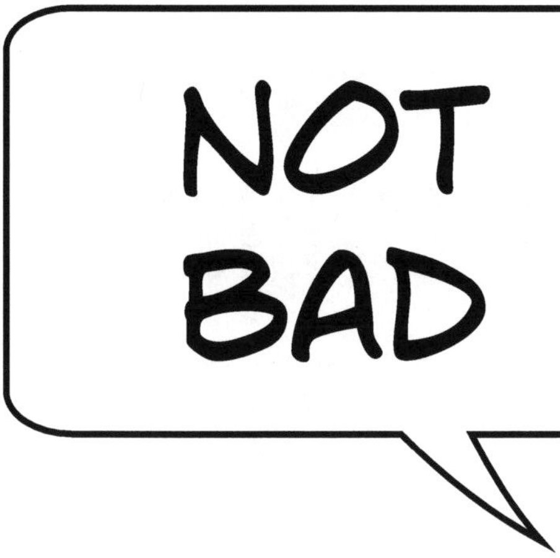
NOT BAD

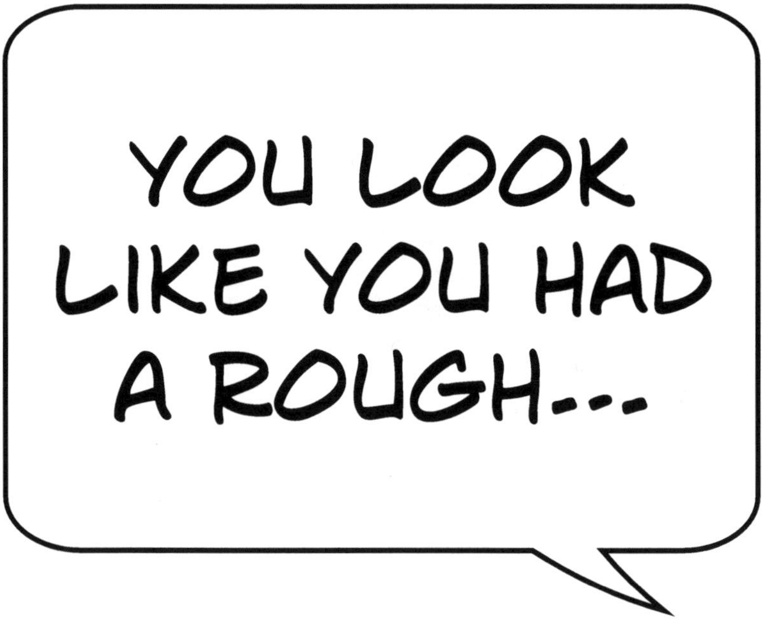
YOU LOOK LIKE YOU HAD A ROUGH...

I CAN'T- MY HOROSCOPE SAID...

LOOKING TO CONNECT WITH LIKE-MINDED...

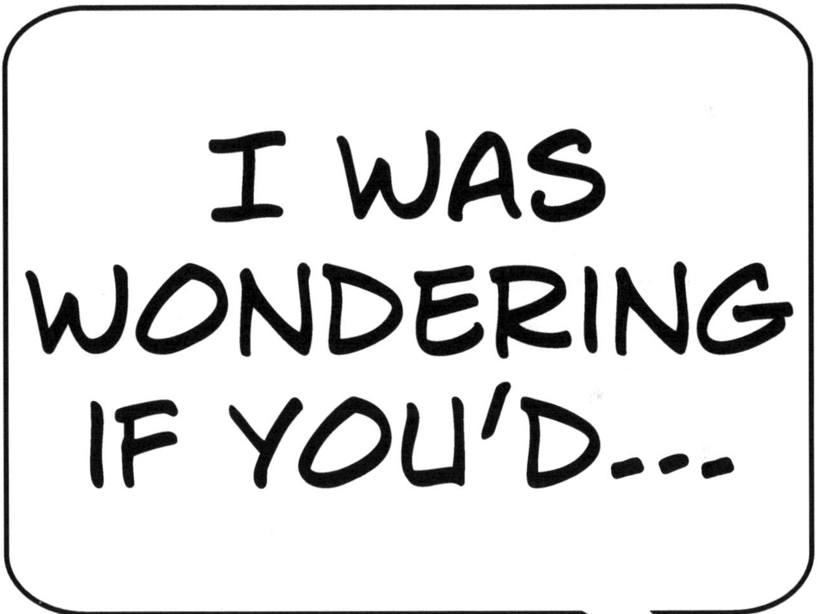
I WAS WONDERING IF YOU'D...

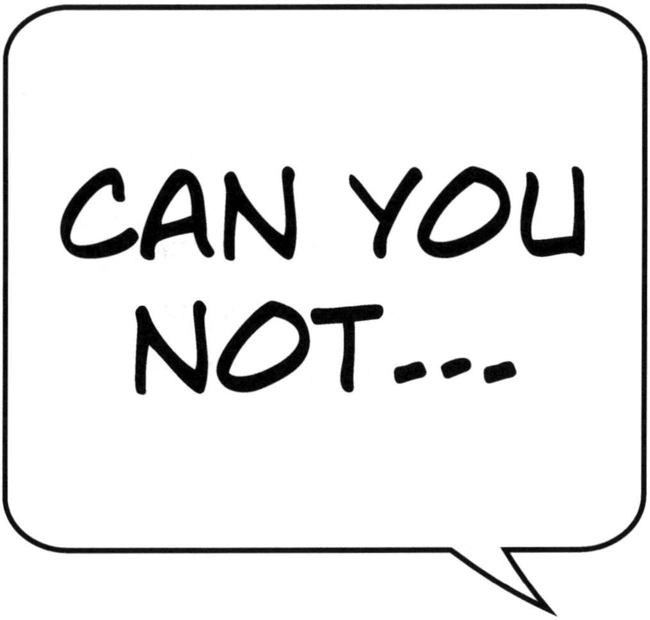
CAN YOU NOT...

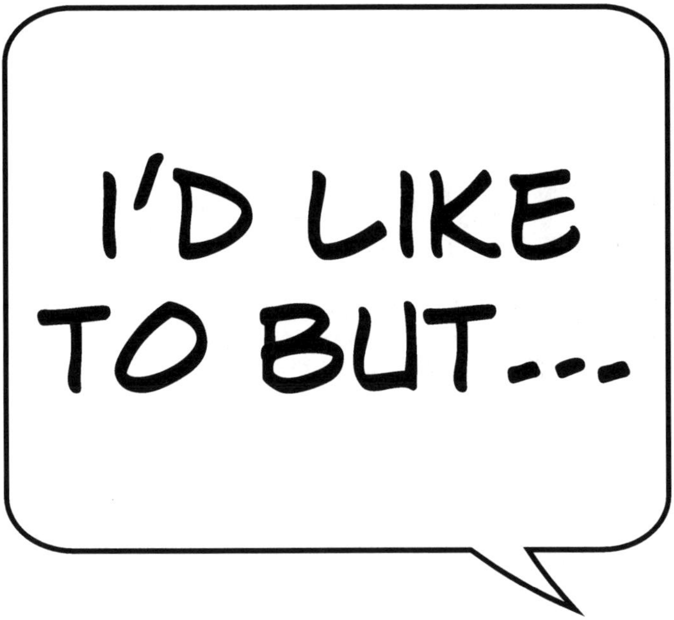
I'D LIKE TO BUT...

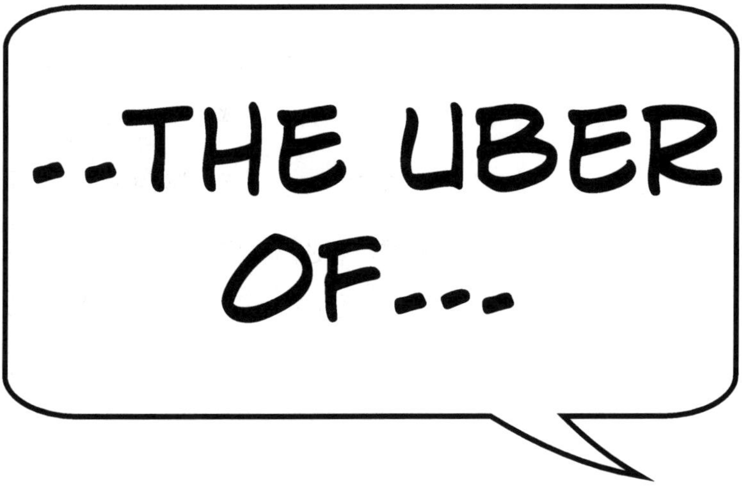
..THE UBER OF...

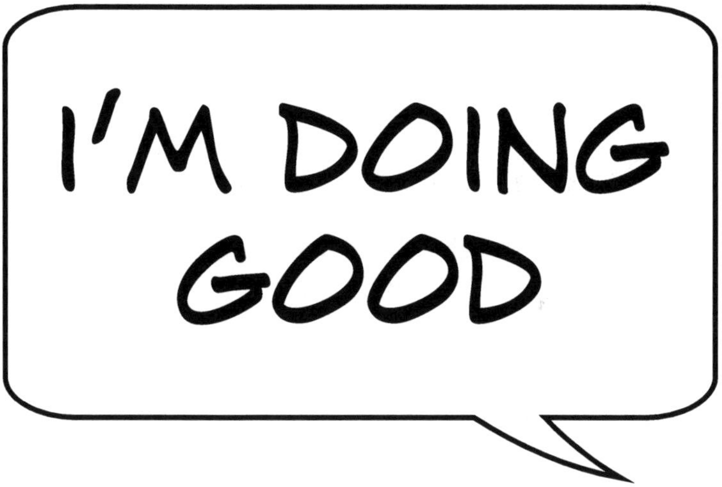
I'M DOING GOOD

ANTITHESIS

ETHOS

If you want to reach me.

TW: @bradgosse
IG: @bradgosse
FB: @bradgosse

Manufactured by Amazon.ca
Bolton, ON

14169850R00133